Draped in Sheer Silk
D0856950
fitted to perfection
Tailored to perfection
All that sparkles and glitters with gold

The Dress

JAN 2015

For Gwyn

All the dresses I've drawn,
and all the dresses I own,
will one day be yours.

The Dress

100 ICONIC MOMENTS IN FASHION

Megan Hess

hardie grant books
MELBOURNE · LONDON

“Over the years I have learned that what is important in a dress is the woman who is wearing it.”

YVES SAINT LAURENT

Contents

Introduction

As a fashion illustrator I've drawn thousands of dresses over the years. Many have been memorable for different reasons: a killer cut, an incredible fabric, an intricate design. I've sketched from the front line at some truly memorable fashion shows, where audience members gasped with excitement as the most brilliant dresses sashayed down the runway. I've illustrated them on all kinds of women, from the world's top supermodels, to Academy Award–winning actresses, to the First Lady of the United States.

But of all the dresses I've drawn, there are a select few that stand out from the rest, dresses so remarkable that they are more than just a garment: they define a moment in time.

These dresses may not be the most expensive or exclusive; they may never have been intended for greatness, but something happened when they were worn. They transformed from a mere garment into a momentous occasion. They became iconic.

This book is a celebration of all the dresses that have made my heart sing – some ridiculous, some shocking and some so beautiful that they literally took my breath away.

01 /

Desig

ners

2012

Versace

There's no designer quite like Versace. Atelier Versace's Fall 2012 couture show during Paris Fashion Week took place at the illustrious Ritz Hotel. As befits such a location, the collection was decadent. The glitter-heavy designs were chic and devilishly sexy, featuring corseted bodices and metallic fabrics in rose gold, blush and purple. The longer evening gowns were constructed from billowing chiffon, exposing models' legs as they sashayed down the catwalk. Christina Hendricks, Milla Jovovich and other fashion heavyweights lined the front row while Donatella Versace made her appearance in a signature black, embellished body-con number and sky-high heels. Like the designer herself, this pink gown stole the show and left everyone in the room craving their own little piece of that Versace magic.

Versace
All that sparkles and glitters with gold

Armani
Delicate Lace
Cate Blanchett

2013

Armani

The Armani Privé Fall 2013 collection, titled *Nude*, featured this incredible gown. Designed by Giorgio Armani, the collection was Old Hollywood meets classic minimalism, and was elegance through and through. One reviewer described it as 'Old Hollywood reborn ... it was hard to tell where fabric ended and skin began. That illusion was unusually sensuous for this designer,' while Armani said that all he wanted for the collection was 'to make women feel beautiful'. And he accomplished this superbly. Cate Blanchett wore the dress to the 2014 Golden Globes, where she made everyone's best-dressed lists and won Best Actress for her role in *Blue Jasmine*. The actor styled her look with Jimmy Choo 'Esam' pumps, Chopard diamond earrings, a faux bob and magenta-tinted lips. When Hollywood's best actress wears the season's most coveted dress, it's a match made in heaven.

2012

Valentino

When I think of Valentino, I think of the ultimate red dress, long, seductive and draped to perfection. Valentino's Summer 2012 show at Paris Fashion Week was truly stunning. The collection was inspired by the revolutionary spirit of early-twentieth-century Mexico, with American artist Georgia O'Keeffe and Italian photographer and political activist Tina Modotti serving as muses. With customary flair, Valentino's creative directors Maria Grazia Chiuri and Pierpaolo Piccioli combined feminine silhouettes with hand-painted floral prints and lace appliqués inspired by Mexican folk embroidery. The make-up was simple and the models' Grecian sandals added to the folkloric mood.

Valentino
Layers and layers of silk

Gold
Lame
toga.
Kate
Moss
Marc
Jacobs

2009

Marc Jacobs

What I love about Marc Jacobs is that you can never predict what he'll create next. He is the master of reinvention and this dress is no exception. All eyes were on Kate Moss in 2009 as she arrived at the *Model as Muse* gala at the MoMA Costume Institute in New York wearing the asymmetric, gold silk-blend lamé creation with a draped finish. The thigh-skimming frock featured a sash on one side and low, open back with a knotted shoulder band. The style icon and supermodel not only co-chaired the event with Justin Timberlake and Marc Jacobs, she also helped to design her look. The always-adventurous Moss worked with famous British milliner Stephen Jones to create a high-gloss turban to match her dress. And to finish the ensemble off, she topped the turban with Shaun Leane's 'White Light' brooch, made with more than two thousand diamonds.

2013

Saint Laurent

When I first saw this ensemble gliding down the runway I think I might have stopped breathing. The dress, with its pussy-bow neckline, side slit and accented leather cummerbund, appeared in one of Hedi Slimane's first collections for Saint Laurent (known previously as Yves Saint Laurent), and it was nothing short of spectacular. Designers Marc Jacobs, Alber Elbaz, Azzedine Alaïa, Vivienne Westwood and Diane von Furstenberg gathered at Paris's Grand Palais to watch the highly anticipated ready-to-wear show. The collection had a distinct 1970s vibe, with models in wide-brimmed hats and platform pumps, while bell sleeves, stacked bracelets and tassel necklaces prevailed throughout. This gown brought the Wild West to the present day and combined everything we love about Saint Laurent with the surge of a new aesthetic.

Sheer Black
with Vintage
Lace
Saint
Laurent

Sheer Tulle.
Dramatic Black
Alexander
Mc Queen

2012

Alexander McQueen

This dramatic black dress comes from Alexander McQueen's critically lauded Pre-fall 2012 collection, designed by creative director Sarah Burton. The extravagance of the design inspired comparisons to Charles Frederick Worth, fashion's first couturier. As Style.com critic Tim Blanks declared, 'This was grand McQueen, the kind of museum-worthy stuff that sustains the legend with its almost operatic lavishness. Burton does it brilliantly.' Burton's modern take on the peplum departed from the traditional pencil-skirt silhouette. 'There was still a flavor of McQueen drama, but the taste was fresh. It left you wanting a whole lot more,' wrote Blanks.

In her research, Burton was influenced by everything from Spanish and Romani art to Victoriana, folk art and 1950s couture. Actress and model Sonam Kapoor wore the dress to the premiere of *Thérèse Desqueyroux* at the 2012 Cannes Film Festival and was described as 'hauntingly beautiful'.

2011

Prada

Miuccia Prada is often dubbed the thinking woman's designer and over the years I have been endlessly inspired by her unpredictable creations. The heiress took over her family's business in 1978 and has invigorated the brand with her contemporary take on beauty and femininity. Her intelligent approach to fashion promotes luxurious, yet functional, design. Gwyneth Paltrow sported this gorgeous pink creation with organza bow detail to the Venice Film Festival in 2011. Paltrow, who has a longstanding relationship with the house, paired the dress perfectly with Prada's 'Cipria Raso' pale pink hard-case clutch and patent leather 'Vernice' peep-toe platforms. Paltrow arrived at the festival on a luxury vintage speedboat – a true Hollywood moment to which only Prada could do justice.

The sweetest
bow tied
in pale
pink
Prada

Dolce and Gabbana
La Dolce Vita
Floral and lace mixed to perfection

2012

Dolce & Gabbana

Wearing a Dolce & Gabbana dress is like escaping to a romantic Italian paradise. The designer's signature mix of leopard, lace and jewels is beyond comparison and its Fall 2012 ready-to-wear show was all about excess – iconic Italian style at its best. Above the runway hung chandeliers draped with vines and roses, and an opulent golden mirror stood as the centrepiece at the fore. Designer Domenico Dolce drew inspiration from his native Sicily and was influenced by its baroque spiritual rituals. There were white communion-like dresses, elaborate capes, and a final parade of corset tops, black lace coats and lavish skirt-suits brocaded with metallic gold thread. As Stefano Gabbana once said, 'We're not about minimalism, we're massimalismo.' The show was acclaimed by all in attendance, including front-row guests Anna Dello Russo, Monica Bellucci and Dame Helen Mirren.

2009

Lanvin

This daring, poofy creation from Lanvin's 2009 line-up at Paris Fashion Week – styled lucidly with nude heels and slicked-back hair – crowned a dazzling Spring collection from Alber Elbaz, who unveiled a series of ruched satin cocktail dresses in yellow, pink, blue, red, plum and other jewel tones. As British *Vogue*'s Alexandra Shulman noted, '[Elbaz] has invented a house style that people really want to wear: classic, feminine, unique and actually practical.' The eye-popping designs and their buoyant silhouettes had the audience in raptures. As an illustrator, seeing this collection unfold on the runway was so inspiring. And as for Alber Elbaz, his own illustrations are as iconic as the dresses he creates.

Ballooning
Sleeves
Lanvin

Leopard
Print
Sheer Silks
Roberto
Cavalli

2013

Roberto Cavalli

I've always thought of Roberto Cavalli as the master of resort style. If you're somewhere fabulous by the water with a glass of champagne, you really should be wearing Cavalli. Olivia Palermo looked a vision in this animal print Cavalli creation at the 2013 amfAR Cinema Against AIDS Gala in France. The one-shoulder cut-out dress featured a flirty, almost hip-high split and a glimpse of waist. Sergio Rossi sandals and a box clutch completed Palermo's look. At the event, the starlet sat at a table hosted by her dressmaker and was joined by Kylie Minogue and Sharon Stone. The designer later hosted an intimate dinner on his yacht, with guests such as Palermo, Stone, Minogue, and models Alessandra Ambrosio and Anja Rubik stepping aboard for a night spent sailing the high-fashion seas.

2012

Tom Ford

When Eva Green stepped out in this high-necked, full-length, smoky-silver gown at the Los Angeles premiere of Tim Burton's gothic comedy *Dark Shadows*, she turned heads. The enigmatic dress, from Tom Ford's Fall 2012 collection, was not shown at London Fashion Week that year. Instead, the industry's top editors and stylists viewed the collection in a private showroom walk-through. A sparkling reptilian crust – real snake and crocodile scales applied individually to the stretch-silk jersey – embellished its skirt, neck and sleeves. Elle Macpherson and Anne Hathaway also attended events in this skin-tight frock, showing off their svelte physiques.

Tom
Ford
TOM FORD

fitted to perfection
Chanel
Couture

2009

Chanel

Of all the dresses in the world, nothing makes my heart sing quite like Chanel couture. It's the history, the craftsmanship, the tweed! Chanel's couture shows are always quite the spectacle and sketching at one is like being at the Olympics for Fashion Illustration. Its Fall 2009 presentation in Paris was no exception. Much to the delight of the crowd, which included Victoria and Vanessa Traina, Keira Knightley and Mario Testino, eccentric creative director Karl Lagerfeld had models make their catwalk entrance through giant Chanel No. 5 bottles. At the time, Lagerfeld had just finished designing Elena Glurdjidze's ballet costume for *The Dying Swan*, which appears to have influenced the ruffle- and tulle-heavy collection. It was highly acclaimed and nothing short of spectacular – a collection that Coco herself would have been proud to send down the runway.

2012

Dior

Wearing a Dior dress is a little like falling in love; it's intoxicating, it makes you dizzy. Dior's Spring 2012 haute couture show marked Bill Gaytten's second year as Acting Creative Director for Dior. An exacting responsibility, but the designer managed to stun audiences and impress critics with this beautiful collection. Gaytten went understated and classic for the collection – but with a twist. 'It's meant to be X-ray Dior,' he said after the show. 'All the structure of iconic Dior, thanks to lots of fittings, but all of it see-through.'

Charlize Theron, long affiliated with Dior, wore this dress to the 2012 Golden Globes. The elegant star accessorised her frock with Givenchy sandals, Cartier diamonds and a vintage Cartier headband. When I first saw this dress, the famous Christian Dior quote sprang to mind: 'tones of grey, pale turquoise and pink will always prevail.'

Dior
Couture
Draped in
Sheer Silk

Black lace
Sheer tulle.
Fendi

2009

Fendi

During the Spring 2009 ready-to-wear season, Karl Lagerfeld presented his collection for Fendi to a power-packed front row, including Anna Wintour, Emmanuelle Alt and Carine Roitfeld. This collection largely adhered to prevailing trends – pale colours, transparent fabrics and bouncy crinoline skirts – but embodied Lagerfeld's own unique approach. The man behind the brand's celebrated double-F logo established a modernist, cinch-waisted silhouette and constructed garments out of broderie anglaise, tablecloth lace and laser cut-outs. This creation, modelled by Sigrid Agren, featured a high neckline and sculpted skirt. Of all the pieces in the collection, the dress stole the show and embodied what Fendi is adored for: elegance with a touch of drama.

1976

Diane von Furstenberg

'Simplicity and sexiness, that's what people want. At a price that's not outrageous', Diane von Furstenberg told Vogue in 1976, the year she was profiled in *Newsweek*. On the news magazine's cover, the designer appeared in the slinky printed wrap dress she built her empire on in the 1970s. The legendary dressmaker invented the iconic frock in 1972 and has been inspiring women like myself ever since. Its easy-to-wear jersey style proved so popular among working women that it is credited with 'bringing back' the dress and causing pantsuits to gradually fall out of fashion. Von Furstenberg, who recommends that women wear her wrap dress sans underwear said, 'They're comfortable, so you're comfortable, you act comfortable, and you get laid.' No wonder it became a symbol for the sexual revolution!

The Wrap dress.
Diane von Fürstenberg

Beaded and detailed to perfection
Paris
Givenchy
haute Couture

2011

Givenchy

In another life, I wear Givenchy dresses morning, noon and night because they're the designs that dreams are made of. When asked about his inspiration for the Givenchy Fall 2011 couture collection, Riccardo Tisci simply replied 'purity'. 'I try to find the light in the darkness,' he said. 'Very pure and soft and fragile; a romantic dream'. The sublime collection comprised only ten items, but took six months to construct – revealing of the effort and detail that went into each piece.

Tisci believes that the magic of couture is born from a garment's first construction in calico, so he stuck to a beige and ivory palette to evoke the whites of the pale cotton used for toiles. The designer employed an extremely delicate technique, working with Chantilly lace, wispy feathers and delicate silk tulle to create ten truly breathtaking gowns.

2011

Mary Katrantzou

This ensemble was unveiled as part of Mary Katrantzou's debut solo show at London Fashion Week. Lovingly named 'Le Meurice' and 'Dorchester', the blouse and skirt feature the designer's signature mixed prints and the padded skirt is sculpted to suggest an antique lampshade. Giant candelabra and chandelier necklaces added to the surreal effect. Katrantzou created a dazzling spectacle at the former Eurostar Terminal catwalk at Waterloo Station, colouring it with her computer-generated trompe l'oeil landscapes. 'With this collection, I wanted to put the room on the woman, rather than the woman in the room,' Katrantzou said after the show. Anna Dello Russo was later spotted in a few pieces from the collection, including this dress, which she wore with a feathered pink fascinator and peep-toe pumps. To me, Mary Katrantzou is a true innovator. Owning one of her dresses is like owning a piece of wearable art.

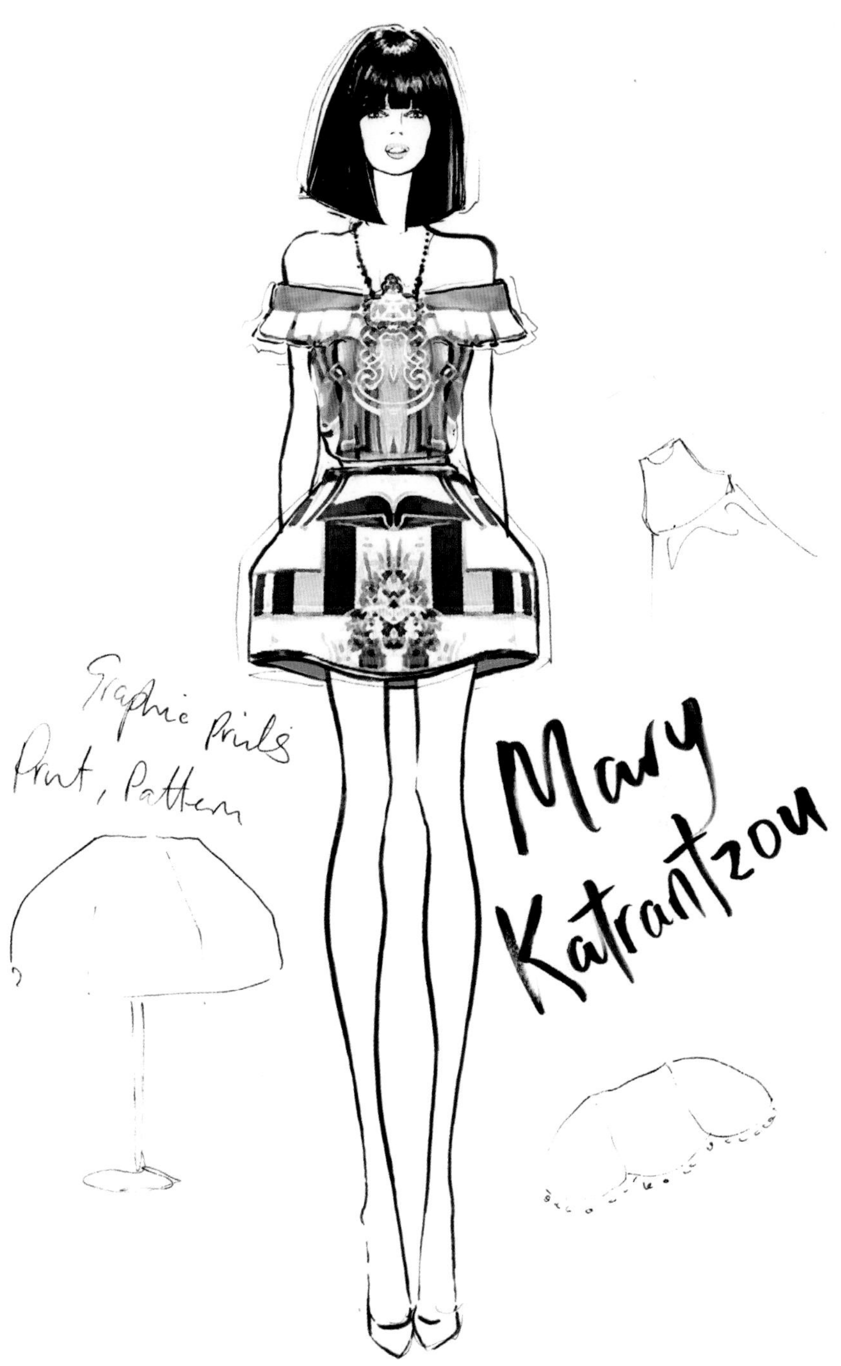
Graphic Prints
Print, Pattern
Mary Katrantzou

Soft peach and nude.
Chloé

2009

Chloé

Anja Rubik and Anna Dello Russo took front-row seats at Espace Ephémère Tuileries in 2009 to see Chloé's highly anticipated Fall ready-to-wear collection. This was Hannah MacGibbon's second year as creative director for the brand, and many were keenly anticipating the show. MacGibbon delivered a collection inspired by the easy glamour of the early 1980s. Think big blanket coats, fluid, high-waisted pants, wrap belts and luscious yet sassy evening wear. Her nude silk-chiffon dresses gathered at the neck and fell low at the back – a very Parisian feel and testament to MacGibbon's dressmaking skills. There's something about Chloé that makes me want to run through a field of tulips with loose, flowing hair. This particular dress captures that sentiment perfectly.

2011

Gucci

For Gucci's Fall 2011 ready-to-wear show at Milan Fashion Week, designer Frida Giannini cited two key influences: Anjelica Huston, as depicted by the photographer Bob Richardson, and Florence Welch of Florence and the Machine. The collection was 'hippie chic', but with the lush, glamorous touches Gucci is known for. The models wore pussy-bow blouses, velvet blazers, snug sweater vests, fedoras decorated with feathers, and colourful shrugs made from hand-dyed silk flowers. For evening wear, Giannini created draped gowns using swathes of chiffon. These seductive dresses were deftly revealing, featured thigh-high slits and were completely sheer, with the models' briefs on full view. I love that a Gucci dress is always a little bit risqué – it is distinctive and exceptional and makes you want to wear it over and over again.

Gucci
Sheer flowers

Floating Sheer
Layered in Lace and delicate beading
Marchesa

2011

Marchesa

A Marchesa piece is like the fairytale dress you dreamed of as a little girl and can now wear as a woman. The label held its Spring 2011 show at Chelsea Art Museum in New York for a crowd packed with Hollywood stars and members of the fashion elite. The largely oriental-inspired collection featured light-as-air gowns with origami folds, cascading fabrics and sweeping precision curves. One of the collection's more whimsical looks, this white, pleated organza mini-shift was accessorised with a matching jade-green clutch and heels. Designers Georgina Chapman and Keren Craig didn't skimp on embellishment, decorating the dress with an intricate beaded bodice and fabulously frothy ruffles at the hem. Each piece in the ultra-feminine collection was both delicate and decadent – dresses fit for the ultimate fairytale.

2008

Nina Ricci

A Nina Ricci dress is cut like no other. Olivier Theyskens went high-drama for the label at Paris Fashion Week in 2008. The designer was influenced by the night: 'I was thinking of a nocturnal mood … something moonlit – a bit magical'. There was a theatrical beauty to the long parade of floating trains and spiky, cryptic shapes that came down the runway. This glittering black dress, worn with towering platform boots, possessed Thierry Mugler–inspired shoulders and a sheer train. The show was exquisite, ethereal and highly personal for Theyskens, given it was his final hurrah for the label. The designer took a long bow at the end while the crowd honoured him with a standing ovation.

Nina
Ricci
Paris

Halston
Metallic pleats.

EARLY 1970s

Halston

When I think of the ultimate 1970s party dress, I think of Halston. Roy Halston Frowick did glossy disco glamour like nobody else. The designer gained a cult-like following among women such as Bianca Jagger, Anjelica Huston and Liza Minnelli, who would appear at Studio 54 wearing his luxurious dresses. This gold, one-shouldered lamé maxi dress features hundreds of semi-sheer pleats. Although modest, its angled neckline and anchoring at the shoulder hint at the potential for nudity and allude to classical Greek attire. The genius of the gown's construction is witnessed in the shape of its fall, while the lustrous fabric shimmers in all the right places. If there were ever a dress that makes you want to dance, this is it.

2010

Moschino

What girly-girl can resist a spot of Moschino's signature cherry print? For its Spring 2010 ready-to-wear show, the fashion house delivered a playful collection. Among the stand-outs was this dress, with its high neckline, bubble-hem skirt and deliciously fruity pattern. Prints of watercolour sunflowers and pastel fruit added to the fun of the collection. And for the finale, party frocks comprised of motley prints were accompanied by beaded garlands and bangles, gold hoop earrings and heart-box hats. Blair Waldorf from *Gossip Girl* wore this design in the first episode of season four, 'Belles de Jour'. The thing I love most about Moschino is the label's sense of humour. Beautifully crafted dresses that come with a wink!

Moschino
Mickey Ears!

Louis
Vuitton
bunny
Ears
Marc
Jacobs

2009

Louis Vuitton

For Louis Vuitton's Fall ready-to-wear show in 2009, Marc Jacobs said he was inspired by 'all the great, elegant Parisian women, like Loulou de la Falaise'. Such quintessential French whimsy manifested in the collection's short hemlines and quirky accessories. This dress, worn by model Uliana Tikhova, featured a blush-coloured tulip skirt and shoulder panels, delightfully paired with the collection's signature bunny ears. Only Jacobs could put huge bunny ears on a grown woman and make it look completely chic. The runway show started seven minutes late (which is actually pretty early for fashion week!) and many important people missed the beginning. Thankfully, the presentation was staged in a clear tent in the Louvre courtyard, allowing passers-by and late editors to witness the spectacle from outside.

1967

Balenciaga

A true fashion innovator, Cristóbal Balenciaga radically altered the fashionable silhouettes of women in the mid-twentieth century. His knowledge of technique and construction and his unflinching perfectionism saw him create garments never before seen in Europe. His popularity grew during the Second World War and women would risk crossing the continent just to get their hands on one of Balenciaga's celebrated square coats. Unique colour combinations, such as black and brown or black lace over bright pink, quickly became his signature. This amazing four-sided cocktail dress first appeared in *Harper's Bazaar*. With its cone-like structure, the dress flares upwards and speaks to the designer's brilliant flair for sculpture. This is fashion on par with art.

Balenciaga
Capped
and cut
to perfection

Gala floral
Carolina Herrera

2013

Carolina Herrera

It's hard to pull off huge prints on full-skirted ballgowns but Carolina Herrera does it with aplomb. For her Pre-fall 2013 collection Herrera decorated her gowns with glorious florals. She used a custom-designed compact – inlaid with jewels and gifted to her by her husband – as inspiration for the collection. The floral patterns grounded the designs, yet stood out for their boldness. This structured, strapless dress, featuring cabbage-rose jacquard and a folded, voluminous skirt, was one of Herrera's finest pieces. The collection was typical of the designer, who describes her style as 'ladylike'. 'I prefer clothes that are simple, well-cut, but with one major extravagance,' she says. Lucy Liu wore the dress to the 2013 Golden Globes, pairing it with a side braid and Lorraine Schwartz earrings to complement the décolletage.

2012

Ralph Lauren

Ralph Lauren's Spring 2012 show at New York Fashion Week presented the designer's modern take on *The Great Gatsby*. Lauren created the costumes for the 1974 film adaptation of F. Scott Fitzgerald's novel, starring Robert Redford and Mia Farrow, inspiring a jazz-age trend at the time. In the lead-up to the release of Baz Luhrmann's remake, the designer took the opportunity to visit the roaring twenties once again. This floor-length, beaded number with a feathered skirt was modelled by Jourdan Dunn and was one of the most striking looks in the collection. On the runway, it was paired with a jewelled cap, an unmistakable throwback to 1920s style. When I first saw this dress, I loved that it felt at once vintage and modern. Not an easy thing to achieve, unless you're Ralph Lauren.

Ralph Lauren
Silver beading and feathers

Missoni
Iconic
Italian

2009

Missoni

Every woman needs a Missoni zigzag in her wardrobe, don't you think? For her decadent Spring 2009 show at Milan Fashion Week, designer Angela Missoni clothed her models in a spectrum of gold. Slight variations of rose and olive green were so subtle that these could merely have been a change in catwalk lighting. The iconic Missoni zigzag took centre stage – reworked in shades of tan and brown and whipped into strapless one-piece swimsuits and draped frocks cinched at the waist with wide leather obi belts. As one reviewer for *Vogue* said, 'This is a woman who knows what she wants and where to get it, and she doesn't care how much it costs.' A true Missoni collector doesn't stop at dresses – she furnishes her entire home with the signature print. After all, a Missoni world is a very nice place to be.

2011

Emilio Pucci

This dress, featuring that legendary bold and jaunty print, is classic Pucci through and through. With its deep-V neckline, it exudes sex appeal despite the floor-grazing length and full sleeves. It was part of the collection designed by Peter Dundas for Emilio Pucci's Fall 2011 show at Milan Fashion Week. The designer embraced loud and vibrant patterns, baroque embellishments and form-fitting bodices to create clothes for women who want to turn heads. English model and socialite Poppy Delevingne wore this dress at London's Serpentine Gallery for the Burberry Summer Party – and critics have called it one of her best fashion moments to date. You really can't go wrong with a Pucci dress. Nothing says confidence more than walking into a room in a dramatic Pucci print.

Pucci

The Beautiful Stripe
Oscar de la Renta

2013

Oscar de la Renta

I've always been partial to a good stripe but this dress took it to another level. One of the highlights of Oscar de la Renta's acclaimed show at New York Fashion Week in 2013 was this black and white striped creation. The silk and duchess satin gown, with its voluminous skirt, evokes the grandeur and glamour of golden-age Hollywood, while the happy nautical stripes add an element of playfulness. Every aspect of the dress is a technical feat – from the underwire bust to the detachable underskirt and hidden pockets. Though Oscar de la Renta is known for his graceful designs, surprises were planned for the show. Along with the occasional latex detail, Cara Delevingne strutted out in a shocking pink dress with pink-streaked hair. At the end of the day, every girl really should have one Oscar de la Renta piece hanging in her wardrobe.

02 /

Icons

1961

Jacqueline Kennedy

Setting a new standard for glamour and style in the White House, Jacqueline Kennedy wore this gorgeous two-toned gown by Chez Ninon to a state dinner honouring President Manuel Prado of Peru on 19 September 1961. Kennedy posed for an official photograph in the black velvet and yellow silk-satin evening dress beside the Peruvian president's fashionable wife, who looked elegant in Dior. Founded by Nona McAdoo Park and Sophie Meldrim Shonnard, Chez Ninon was Kennedy's exclusive go-to salon for American-made, French-inspired pieces. Chez Ninon created Kennedy's iconic pink wool suit and pillbox hat, although the outfit is often mistaken for Chanel.

Jacqueline
Kennedy

Anna
Dello Russo
Oscar de
La Renta
VOGUE
Pink
feathers

2013

Anna Dello Russo

Anna Dello Russo is like catnip for street-style bloggers. The editor-at-large for *Vogue* Japan stepped out of the 2013 men's shows in Milan wearing this plumed fuchsia ensemble by Oscar de la Renta and reflective shades. The dress was straight from the runway, where Cara Delevingne modelled it with a crystal belt earlier in the season. It wasn't the first time Dello Russo had proven by example that grown women can wear pink: the eccentric trendsetter was snapped wearing a sparkly watermelon headpiece at New York Fashion Week in 2011. The attention-grabbing fascinator was created by Piers Atkinson and commissioned by Alan Journo. As this look demonstrates, Dello Russo never takes herself too seriously – which makes her perfect for style-stalking and, of course, the ultimate artistic muse!

2009

Michelle Obama

One of the most incredible commissions that I've ever received was to draw Michelle Obama in this dress. Barack Obama summed it up perfectly when he asked the crowd at his first presidential inaugural ball: 'First of all, how good-looking is my wife?' Michelle Obama, indeed, looked stunning in the draped, one-shoulder chiffon ball gown covered in feathery appliqués and beading by Jason Wu, who only found out that the First Lady was wearing his design when he saw her on television. The white dress was equal parts glamorous and youthful, with a touch of period charm evoking the stately ball gowns of 1950s designers like Christian Dior and Jacques Fath. To add to the opulence, it was adorned with thousands of Swarovski crystals.

Jason Wu.
Michelle Obama

Twiggy
The Shot Dress
Fuchsia Pink

1966

Twiggy

The unmistakable face of the swinging sixties, Lesley Lawson, known as Twiggy, has been a style icon for over four decades. Known for her shift dresses, spidery lashes and sleek parted hairdo, her gamine look came to define the decade. Discovered when she was only sixteen, Twiggy was hired to model for London designer Mary Quant, who is credited with popularising the miniskirt. This illustration, depicting the English model in Quant's bubblegum shift, is based on a photograph taken in the studio in 1966. Oh Twiggy, how we love that playful pout!

1968

Brigitte Bardot

Brigitte Bardot's coquettish attitude and smouldering beauty made her a legend, and her on-screen wardrobe garnered just as much attention. For the 1968 Western adventure *Shalako*, Bardot worked with London designer Cynthia Tingey, who also created period costumes for *The Vikings* and *Genghis Khan*. Bardot played French countess Irina Lazaar and required stylish clothes fit for the arid landscape of a Western. This gorgeous string-tie blouse and layered skirt, worn with heeled boots, was one of the film's most striking looks. Due to timing overlaps, Bardot was unable to appear in the Bond film *On Her Majesty's Secret Service*. Coincidentally, however, she starred opposite Sean Connery in *Shalako*. The only accessory that almost outshone her outfit was the famous Bardot hair.

Brigitte
Bardot
white
Western
Chic

Bianca Jagger
STUDIO 54
Dramatic Red.
Disco.

1970s

Bianca Jagger

How outrageously decadent is this ensemble? Bianca Jagger was a regular at legendary nightclub Studio 54 and would frequently wear Halston creations on the dance floor. The guest list often included Andy Warhol, Debbie Harry and Anjelica Huston – celebrities who came to define the nightclub movement – but it was Bianca Jagger who put the New York hotspot on the map. In this look, Jagger wears a ravishing sequinned gown with halter neckline and matching red beret. Together, Jagger and Roy Halston helped shape 1970s style. His designs were sometimes ostentatious, but always chic and wearable, and never forgettable.

2003

Kate Moss

Kate Moss channelled heritage glamour in this lemon chiffon frock, which she picked up from Los Angeles vintage store Lily et Cie. The style icon was photographed wearing it on a night out in New York in 2003. Though pale yellow is usually tricky to pull off, Moss styled the dress to perfection – and inspired a thousand copycats around the globe. The world's most stylish model looked every bit the Hollywood golden girl in the prom dress with off-the-shoulder detail and a youthful knee-high hem. The frock was a surprising choice, given that the supermodel usually favours black-on-black and skinny jeans. It was such a hit, in fact, that two years later Moss created a replica for her first Topshop collection. Of course, we were all lining up outside the store to buy one for ourselves.

Kate Moss

Teal Flang Gown
Princess Kate

2012

Catherine, Duchess of Cambridge

Attending the London Olympic Gala Concert in 2012, the former Kate Middleton stepped gracefully onto the red carpet at Royal Albert Hall in this lace-bodice, cap-sleeved dress by one of her favourite designers, Jenny Packham. The pleated teal frock was a modified version of the 'Aspen' gown from the designer's Spring 2012 collection and featured a flowing silk-chiffon skirt and Swarovski-beaded belt. The Duchess of Cambridge, who often leaves Kensington Palace to shop at Packham's flagship boutique in Mayfair, paired the frock with Jimmy Choo 'Vamp' high-heeled sandals, an elegant chignon and matching bespoke clutch. Even on a mere mortal this dress would be beautiful, but on the Duchess, it was mesmerising.

1994

Elizabeth Hurley

Gianni Versace's iconic safety-pin dress made Elizabeth Hurley a household name in 1994. Everyone, from your nan and mum to your postman, remembers seeing her step out at the premiere of *Four Weddings and a Funeral*. The black cocktail dress was made with pieces of silk and lycra, with six oversized gold safety pins used to fasten the dress in 'strategic places', celebrating the female form. The dangerously sexy dress not only upstaged her famous boyfriend Hugh Grant, it upstaged the entire event and made Hurley an instant global star. Hurley said that the dress was a favour from Versace because she couldn't afford to buy one of their dresses. 'His [Grant's] people told me they didn't have any evening wear, but there was one item left in their press office. So I tried it on and that was it.'

Versace
Elizabeth
Hurley

VOGUE
Carine Roitfeld
Black Lace.

2011

Carine Roitfeld

With her penchant for lace, leather and black, former French *Vogue* editor and *CR Fashion Book* founder Carine Roitfeld always dresses with a certain *je ne sais quoi*, and the outfit she wore to De Grisogono's tenth birthday at the Cannes Film Festival in 2011 was no exception. The jeweller hosted a stellar party with heavyweight guests such as Leonardo DiCaprio, Roberto Cavalli and Heidi Klum in attendance. The event's theme was Boho Glamour and Roitfeld opted for this sophisticated yet sexy number by Tom Ford. The floor-length design was inspired by lingerie, featuring a detailed bust and black panels of floral lace. Roitfeld always looks amazing in tough leather with a touch of lace, and her best accessory is always her confidence.

2004

Carrie Bradshaw

When Candace Bushnell created Carrie Bradshaw, she created every woman's fairytale heroine. My only question is: how could our heroine be stood up in *that* dress? Carrie Bradshaw (Sarah Jessica Parker) wears the exquisite thousand-layer masterpiece as she waits for the Russian, Petrovsky, in the last episode of *Sex and the City*. The Versace 'Mille Feuille' couture gown – named after the slice made from layers of delicate pastry – retailed at seventy-nine thousand dollars and comprised layer upon layer of delicate tulle and chiffon ruffles in sea-foam green. *Sex and the City*'s costume designer Patricia Field called it one of her favourite pieces in Carrie's wardrobe. For me, this dress was the perfect finale to six seasons of television's greatest fashion moments. Every woman should get to spend at least one afternoon lounging around a Paris hotel suite in this dress.

Carrie Bradshaw
Paris Couture.

Diana
Vreeland

1979

Diana Vreeland

Diana Vreeland once said, 'Too much good taste can be boring' – and she lived her life by that philosophy. The legendary style icon changed the face of fashion, working at *Harper's Bazaar* and *Vogue*, and later becoming a consultant for the Costume Institute at the Metropolitan Museum of Art. This illustration is based on a photo taken by Horst P. Horst in 1979. Vreeland was captured relaxing in her red living room wearing a luxurious metallic ensemble that almost blended into the background. Of the vivid hue, Vreeland wrote, 'Red is the great clarifier – bright, cleansing and revealing. It makes all other colors look beautiful.' The apartment, which Vreeland called her 'garden in hell', was decorated by Billy Baldwin, who was also commissioned by Jacqueline Kennedy to decorate the White House. Not many women can actually own a colour, but to me Vreeland has the last word on red.

1983

Princess Diana

Diana, Princess of Wales, loved her Hachi gown so much she thought it worthy of three repeats! She first wore the white columnar dress with detailed glass beading and crystal embroidery on a royal tour of Australia and New Zealand in 1983. Diana resurrected the gown in Washington, D.C. in 1984, before wearing it during a state visit to Japan – a fitting choice given that Hachi was a Japanese designer. It is considered Diana's first mature dress and marked a departure from her typical 'princess' gowns. *You* magazine purchased the dress in 1997, raising seventy-five thousand dollars for Princess Diana's charities. It was later recreated in miniature form for a Franklin Mint doll modelled in Diana's likeness.

Princess Diana
Hachi
embroidered White Gown
Crystals and delicate beading

Iris Apfel
Canary Yellow
Layers of Vintage Jewels

2011

Iris Apfel

When Iris Apfel walks into a room, everyone notices. The interior designer and New York native is walking, talking proof that you can look fabulous at any age – all it takes is a splash of bold colour and a few choice accessories! When she attended the CFDA Fashion Awards in 2011 – to present Alexander Wang with the award for Accessories Designer of the Year – Apfel wore this bright lemon blouse with her trademark statement jewellery. And of course, no look of hers is complete without those flying-saucer spectacles. Apfel has a knack for accessorising and earlier that year designed a collection of costume jewellery for luxury e-tailer Yoox.

In years to come, I can only dream that I'll have half the sartorial panache that Iris has had her whole life.

03 /

Wedd

ings

1950

Elizabeth Taylor

Elizabeth Taylor would walk down the aisle eight times throughout her life, but it was her first wedding, to Conrad 'Nicky' Hilton, Jr., that begot this celebrated dress. Designed by Hollywood costumier Helen Rose, the gown was inspired by the one Taylor wore in 1950's *Father of the Bride* and took fifteen seamstresses three months to make. Comprising twenty-five yards of ivory satin, it features an inbuilt corset – which cinched Taylor's waist to a tiny twenty inches – and complex pearl beading on the neckline. The eighteen-year-old bride was gifted the dress by Metro-Goldwyn-Mayer, the film studio under which she was contracted. In 2013, the iconic dress sold at a Christie's auction for £121,875 – more than double its maximum estimate.

Elizabeth
Taylor

Grace
Kelly

1956

Grace Kelly

Grace Kelly's 1956 wedding to Prince Rainier III of Monaco was a real-life fairytale. The commoner from Philadelphia marrying a European blue blood had the whole world watching, with women particularly eager to see Kelly's dress. Created by Helen Rose, a costume designer in the wardrobe department of Metro-Goldwyn-Mayer, the gown possessed a lace bodice, delicate veil and two petticoats. It was worth more than seven thousand dollars and its fabrics included twenty-five yards of silk taffeta, one hundred yards of silk tulle, peau de soie and antique Brussels rose-point lace. The princess teamed it with a Juliet cap embroidered with seed pearls and orange blossom. The wedding gown is one of history's most famous and is said to have inspired Kate Middleton's dress over fifty years later.

1953

Jacqueline Kennedy

Jacqueline Bouvier wasn't yet an international style icon when she married John F. Kennedy, but she was already enchanting crowds with her graceful flair. She was the centre of attention marrying the dashing senator at Saint Mary's Church on Rhode Island in 1953. Her dress, designed by African-American dressmaker Ann Lowe, almost never arrived. After months of toil, Kennedy's dress was destroyed in Lowe's workroom when it was flooded ten days before the wedding. Lowe and her staff worked frantically for eight days and nights to deliver the back-up dress on time. It's fortunate that this gown made it down the aisle, because the Kennedy wedding was the social event of the season – and despite her last-minute wardrobe disaster, the bride was resplendent and her dress inspired many emulators.

Jacqueline Kennedy

Carolyn
Bessette
Kennedy
The Slip
Dress
Narciso
Rodriguez
chic
Silk

1996

Carolyn Bessette-Kennedy

Carolyn Bessette-Kennedy will always be remembered for her relaxed, minimalist style – and her wedding dress was no exception. The gown she wore to marry John F. Kennedy, Jr. in a secret ceremony on Cumberland Island, Georgia, epitomised 1990s understatement and 'less is more'. The unadorned, floor-length silk number was designed by Narciso Rodriguez, one of Bessette-Kennedy's closest friends and relatively unknown at the time. An estimated forty thousand dollars and two three-hour couture fittings in Paris were required to perfect the dress. Teamed with a hand-rolled tulle veil, long silk gloves and beaded satin sandals by Manolo Blahnik, the dress is an exemplar of simple and elegant bridalwear.

1981

Princess Diana

On 29 July 1981, Lady Diana Spencer stepped from her horse-drawn carriage wearing a voluminous ivory wedding dress. All eyes were on her as she walked down the aisle with the dramatic twenty-five-foot train made from forty yards of silk taffeta trailing behind her. The designers were David and Elizabeth Emanuel, who had worked long hours decorating the gown with hand embroidery, sequins and ten thousand pearls. The paparazzi swarmed the Emanuels' store, yet every aspect of the gown's design was kept secret – not even the taffeta manufacturers knew what colour it would be as white and cream were both ordered.

In true 1980s style, the frock was totally excessive. In fact, the train was so long that Diana's father John Spencer found it difficult to fit inside the coach to accompany his daughter to the cathedral. That didn't stop the dress from being emulated the world over and just like that, the puffy-sleeve trend was born.

Princess
Diana

Vivienne
Westwood
Carrie
Bradshaw

2008

Carrie Bradshaw

Who could forget the elaborate Vivienne Westwood gown and turquoise feather headpiece that Carrie Bradshaw (Sarah Jessica Parker) wore when Big left her at the altar in the first *Sex and the City* movie? Indeed, the dress was so popular that Westwood created a cocktail version. Worn by Rihanna, Nicola Roberts, Sandra Bullock, Nigella Lawson and Sarah Jessica Parker herself, the casual version was made available from online boutique Net-a-Porter and sold out within hours. Only have eyes for the original? As luck would have it, floor-sweeping versions can be made to order at the Vivienne Westwood boutique in London – provided you've got six months to wait and at least sixteen thousand dollars!

2010

Nicole Richie

Not content with one, Nicole Richie had three Marchesa wedding dresses to get her through her big day. The first dress, which she wore saying 'I do' to Joel Madden, reportedly cost twenty thousand dollars and had an elaborate skirt crafted with more than one hundred yards of hand-draped silk organza and tulle petals. The long-sleeved creation was apparently inspired by Grace Kelly's wedding gown, and its embroidered lace bodice was bound with a wide satin waistband. Unlike Kelly, Richie had a skirt that ingeniously detached to make the dress dance-floor friendly!

Nicole Richie
Marchesa
Layers of tulle

Catherine
Duchess of
Cambridge
McQueen

2011

Catherine, Duchess of Cambridge

The world watched with bated breath as Kate Middleton wed Prince William at Westminster Abbey. Kate's wedding dress was always going to have an impact on style history – seared into our minds and inspiring thousands of knock-offs. Sarah Burton from Alexander McQueen designed the chosen gown, which, with its full skirt and long sleeves, was inevitably traditional. The bodice featured floral lacework, which was appliquéd to tulle by employees at the Royal School of Needlework. To maintain secrecy, the embroiderers at the School were told that the dress was for a television costume drama and that cost was no object. For the 'something blue' element of wedding tradition, a pale blue ribbon was sewn to the gown's interior.

1971

Bianca Jagger

Bianca Jagger was four months pregnant with her daughter Jade when she married Mick Jagger at Saint-Tropez's Hôtel Byblos in 1971. Before the nuptials, the bride-to-be popped into Yves Saint Laurent's headquarters on Rue Spontini and asked him to design her wedding dress. A young student living in Paris, she couldn't afford haute couture so had to settle for his Rive Gauche ready-to-wear designs. Jagger picked a white 'Le Smoking' jacket and skirt, and wore nothing underneath. Saint Laurent also designed the wide-brimmed hat and veil for Jagger's wedding day, and decided that instead of carrying a bouquet, she ought to wear a corsage to match the suit.

Yves
Saint
Laurent
Bianca
Jagger

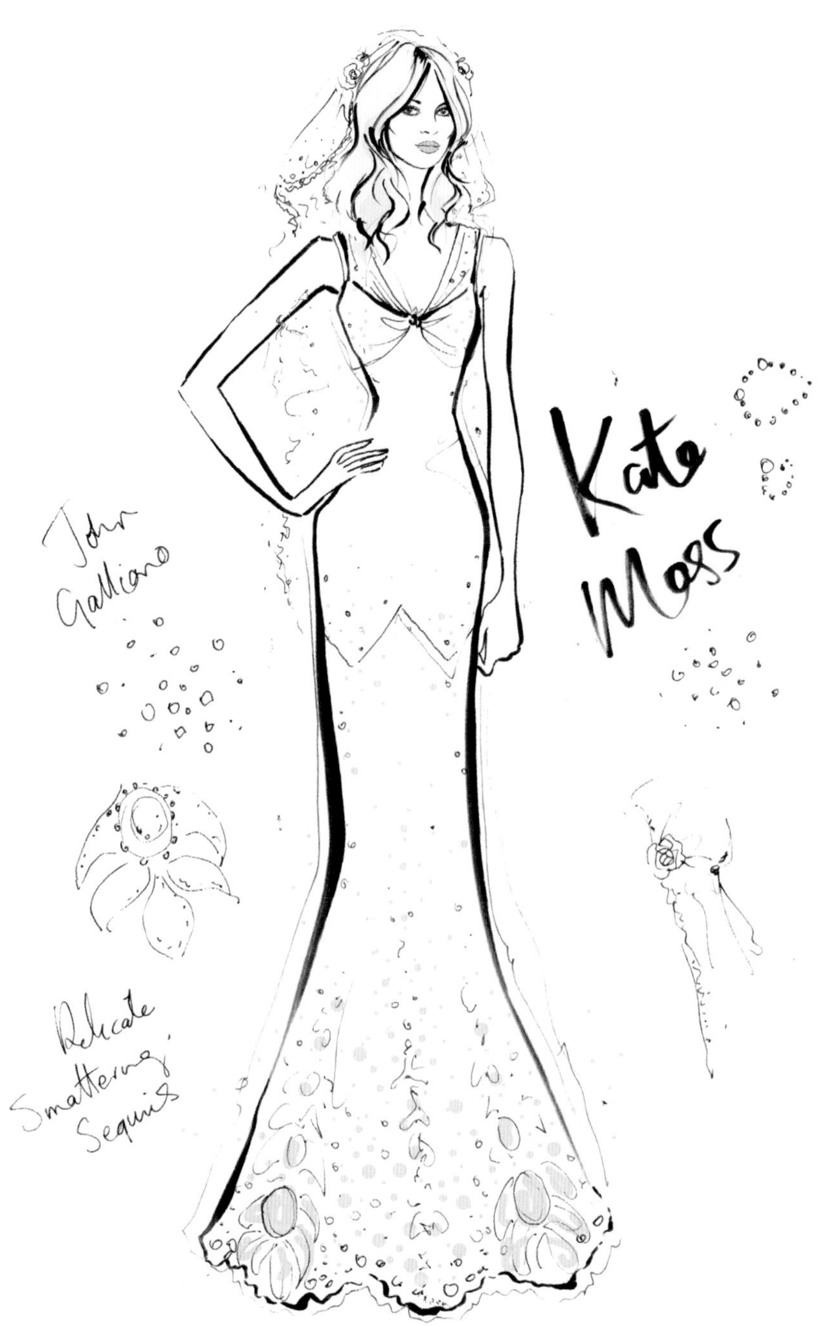
Kate Moss
John Galliano
Delicate Smattering Sequins

2011

Kate Moss

John Galliano was the creative genius behind Kate Moss's bridal dress when she wed long-time beau Jamie Hince at Saint Peter's Church in the village of Southrop. The cream bias-cut dress had a matching floor-length veil and was inspired by *The Great Gatsby*, Moss's favourite book. The vintage-style dress incorporated delicate sheer panelling and was spangled with gold sequins as an extra flourish.

John Galliano was the surprise guest at the midsummer's eve ceremony, and the bride's father Pete even thanked the designer for the 'beautiful dress' during his speech. The guests – which included Stella McCartney, Dame Vivienne Westwood and Stefano Pilati – gave Galliano a standing ovation, while fashion commentators were equally enthusiastic. As British *Vogue*'s Harriet Quick said, 'It was a superb dress and pure Galliano … a tribute to him'.

2010

Vera Wang

As Anthony Marentino, Charlotte's gay bestie on *Sex and the City* says, 'You want pasta, you go to Little Italy. You want wedding, you go Wang.' He couldn't be more right. Vera Wang always dictates bridal trends, making her spring show a must-watch every season. At New York Fashion Week in 2010, the designer sent out this ruffled frock with full skirt and sheer black ribbon. The dress was designed to feature in the wedding photo shoot in the first *Sex and the City* film and is similar to Kate Hudson's dress in the 2009 movie *Bride Wars*. The feathered, feminine design is typical of Wang – fit for any storybook wedding.

Vera
Wang

Oscar de la Renta
Covered in delicate lace

2007

Oscar de la Renta

Jacquetta Wheeler sashayed down the runway at Oscar de la Renta's Spring 2007 ready-to-wear show in New York wearing this gorgeous cap-sleeved gown with lace overlay. Brooke Shields later chose the dress to wear to the 2007 Costume Institute Gala, pairing it with red earrings and a metallic clutch. Oscar de la Renta's show attracted widespread media attention and fashion critics lauded the collection. After the finale, model Tanya Dziahileva delivered a bouquet of flowers to the show's guest of honour, Roger Federer, who was seated in the front row. That year, de la Renta won Designer of the Year at the CFDA Awards. There's something about an Oscar de la Renta dress that makes you feel extraordinary – and what better way to feel on your wedding day.

2013

Chanel

Karl Lagerfeld created quite the stir at Chanel's Spring 2013 couture show in Paris. At the end of the spectacle at the Grand Palais, the designer sent two identical brides down the runway. The models wore ethereal feathered gowns with gothic makeup and downy plumage cascading from their hair. They posed hand-in-hand as an act of support for the proposed gay-marriage laws in France at the time. With the happy couple was four-year-old Hudson Kroenig, the cherubic son of model Brad Kroenig, who was chosen by Lagerfeld to play pageboy for the occasion. It takes an avant-garde bride to wear this couture dress on her wedding day, but if you're going to wear something daring it might as well be Chanel! After the show, Lagerfeld said, 'I don't even understand the debate ... Since 1904 the church and state have been separate.'

Chanel
Wedding Couture
fitted to perfection

04 / Music

2008

Tina Turner

Tina Turner needed a captivating ensemble to mark her 2008 comeback to the stage for her fiftieth-anniversary world tour. After retiring at sixty, it took a conversation with Sophia Loren and Giorgio Armani to convince her to get back in the game. When preparing her stage wardrobe, Turner called upon veteran designer Bob Mackie, whom she had worked with for more than thirty years and who is famous for dressing the Supremes, Liza Minnelli, Cher and Barbra Streisand. Mackie designed this glittering beaded mini-dress, which flaunted Turner's incredible body. The sixty-eight-year-old stunned everyone with her taut physique and powerhouse performance that night. There was and will only ever be one Tina Turner!

Tina Turner
Leopard print
Bob mackie

The Supremes

1969

The Supremes

I must admit, I really wanted to be one of the Supremes, because as well as their immense talent, I coveted their fabulous costumes! The Supremes exuded glamour and sophistication. They performed with grace and confidence, creating a shining example of modern American womanhood during a period of great social change. Diana Ross, Mary Wilson and Florence Ballard purchased their costumes from department stores when they started out, but as their fame grew, so did their budget. Hollywood designer Bob Mackie was called upon to create their dresses for the NBC television special *G.I.T. on Broadway* in 1969. Mackie devised these pink feathered-hem frocks, which were also worn in the back-cover photograph of their album with the Four Tops, *The Return of the Magnificent Seven*. The trio's lavish costumes, embellished with beading and sequins, cost as much as two thousand dollars each – the equivalent of around twenty thousand dollars today.

1984

Madonna

Leave it to Madonna to steal Cyndi Lauper's thunder at the 1984 MTV Video Music Awards. Though Lauper was supposed to be the star that night, Madonna caught everyone's attention when she emerged onstage atop a seventeen-foot-tall wedding cake wearing the same frock from her 'Like a Virgin' music video. Designed by Marisol, the playful 'wedding' dress featured a tutu skirt and veil accessorised with white gloves and the famed 'Boy Toy' belt buckle. No one expected her performance to be so raunchy. Madonna's manager at the time, Freddy DeMann, said of the incident: 'Never again will I let her be shot live.' Largely due to Madonna's provocative dance moves, 1984 has been touted as one of the most memorable years in the history of the VMAs.

Madonna
BOY TOY

Lady
Ga Ga
VMA
The
Meat
Dress

2010

Lady Gaga

Who could forget the frock made out of raw steak that Lady Gaga wore to the 2010 MTV Video Music Awards? Coined the 'meat dress' by the tabloids, it was created by Argentine designer Franc Fernandez and styled by Gaga's close friend and costume mastermind Nicola Formichetti. The meat actually came from Fernandez's family butcher. While accepting the award for Video of the Year from presenter Cher, Gaga joked, 'I never thought I'd be asking Cher to hold my meat purse.' Condemned by animal-rights groups – no surprises there – the meat dress was named the top fashion statement of 2010 by *Time* magazine. Gaga offered her own explanation of the frock, stating, 'If we don't stand up for what we believe in and if we don't fight for our rights, pretty soon we're going to have as much rights as the meat on our own bones.' Taxidermists later preserved the dress, curing it like jerky, before it went on display at the Rock and Roll Hall of Fame in 2011.

2005

Gwen Stefani

As leader of the mid-1990s style pack, it was only natural for Gwen Stefani to branch out and launch her own label. The No Doubt frontwoman founded L.A.M.B. – an acronym of Love Angel Music Baby – in 2003, fusing Guatemalan, Japanese, Indian and Jamaican inspirations. Her outfit at the 2005 MTV Video Music Awards was more pared back than her usual look. Stefani worked leopard print with a demure and ladylike 1950s silhouette. The VMAs was her last event before she went on hiatus to have her first son, Kingston, but the outfit definitely left a lasting impression. At the awards, Stefani and rapper Snoop Dogg won host Sean Combs's 'Diddy Fashion Challenge'. They were awarded fifty thousand dollars to donate to charity.

Gwen Stefani
Leopard Print

Cher

1986

Cher

Cher's singular Bob Mackie masterpiece is one of the most outrageous ensembles ever worn to the Academy Awards. Cher looked every bit the showgirl and stole the spotlight from all other actresses in her dramatic cape-like gown and headpiece, which stood at two feet tall and was made from rooster feathers. Rumour has it that Cher chose the outfit after being told that she wasn't nominated for her 1985 flick *Mask* despite her highly acclaimed performance 'because the Academy doesn't think you're serious [when] you don't dress seriously'. The outré two-piece ensemble perfectly suited her maverick personality and the singer considers it one of her favourite looks to date. Like everything that Cher wears, the outfit would have been a disaster on anyone else, but on the singer it's not only becoming, it's fabulous.

2014

Beyoncé

Though she might not have walked the red carpet at the 56th Annual Grammy Awards, Beyoncé Knowles-Carter still managed to steal the style spotlight. After performing the opening number with Jay Z, the pop diva changed into a sheer panelled gown by *Project Runway* alum Michael Costello. Beyoncé's stylist Ty Hunter, who compiled five dress options for the singer, approached Costello at a Golden Globes afterparty and asked him to make something 'extra special'. The risqué dress that Costello designed was entirely handmade, with a nude mesh underlay to give the illusion of skin. The velvety white damask pattern created the effect of snow falling onto flowers or leaves, and the dress was later showcased in Costello's winter wonderland–themed collection at New York Fashion Week in 2014.

Beyonce
the graphic lace

Blondie
sheer and
pleated silk.

1979

Debbie Harry

Who doesn't love Blondie's karaoke classic, 'Heart of Glass'? The disco song, which appears on their 1979 album *Parallel Lines*, was accompanied by a music video featuring Debbie Harry lip-syncing and making eyes at the camera. The singer wore frosted eye shadow, glossy red lipstick and a silver, asymmetrical one-shoulder dress by Stephen Sprouse. To create the dress, the designer took a photograph of static lines on his television and printed it onto different fabrics. According to Harry, he 'put a layer of cotton fabric underneath and a layer of chiffon on top, and then the scan lines would do this op-art thing'. While many assume that the video was filmed at Studio 54, it was actually filmed at a little-known, now defunct, bar called Copa in New York City.

1985

Grace Jones

Grace Jones's angular silhouette lends itself to the creations of Azzedine Alaïa, the Tunisian-born couturier known for his figure-sculpting, body-enhancing designs. This illustration, depicting Jones in a hooded dress that clings to her svelte form, is based on a photograph taken before an Alaïa runway show in 1985. The two artists worked together throughout their careers. Jones, famed for her glamorous androgyny and avant-garde style, called upon Alaïa to design a range of similar hooded pieces for the Bond film *A View to a Kill*, in which she played the villainess. In October of the same year, when Alaïa won Best Designer at the 'Oscars of Fashion' industry awards in France, Grace Jones carried Alaïa onstage to accept his award in her arms. What more could a designer want than to be carried by the ultimate Bond Villain?

Grace
Jones

Versace
Jennifer Lopez

2000

Jennifer Lopez

We're still talking about the Versace dress that Jennifer Lopez wore to the Grammys in 2000, which was viewed on grammy.com 642,917 times in twenty-four hours. The transparent dress featured a tropical palm and bamboo pattern, citrine brooch and low-cut neckline, which dipped several inches below Lopez's navel. Apparently, the singer had no idea how shocking the dress would be. As the star told *W* magazine, 'When I came on stage with David Duchovny, who was the biggest star in the world then, he said to the audience, "Nobody is looking at me." This loud sound started from the back of the room – it was kind of like a roar, over me in the dress. When I went to my seat, I said, "What's the big deal?!"'

To me, this dress is a perfect example of what Versace does best; nipped, draped and plunging in all the right places.

2013

Diana Ross

Diana Ross is the original diva. The sixty-nine-year-old singer, who is still touring, is known for her soulful music and sophisticated style. As the frontwoman of the Supremes in the 1960s, Ross helped define R & B's legendary Motown Sound and her wildly curly hair and amazing disco wardrobe became her trademarks. Ross studied fashion design and has been known for creating her own costumes since the early days.

One of Ross's more recent designs is this billowing, red tulle boa, worn during her comeback performance at the Hollywood Bowl in 2013. The look was one of five costumes she donned during the short seventy-five-minute performance, with each outfit as colourful as her sound. No wonder her daughter, actress Tracee Ellis Ross, and Mary J. Blige have cited her as their style icon!

Diana Ross

Kylie
Dripping in Gold

2010

Kylie Minogue

From the moment Kylie burst onto our screens twenty-five years ago, her sartorial choices have been a hot topic of conversation. In retrospect, I have loved them all, even the poodle perm and high-waisted acid-wash jeans – and it's her biggest hits and video clips that have made her the fashion icon she is today. Who could forget the white hooded jumpsuit from 'Can't Get You Out of My Head' and those gold thrift-store hotpants in 'Spinning Around'?

For 2010's 'Get Outta My Way', Minogue steamed up our screens in a sculpted bodice dress with gold chain detail by New York design duo the Blonds, teamed with gold Christian Louboutin peep-toe booties. The label also dreamed up the giant claw ring seen in the clip, creating a miniature replica of the entire outfit for a limited-edition Blond Gold Barbie in 2013. You know that your outfit is iconic when Barbie wears it!

05 / Film

Gentlemen Prefer Blondes / 1953

Marilyn Monroe

The show-stopping pink frock that Marilyn Monroe wore singing 'Diamonds Are a Girl's Best Friend' in 1953's *Gentlemen Prefer Blondes* has been etched into our collective memory. Hollywood costume designer William Travilla had originally designed an extravagant showgirl costume for Monroe to wear in this scene, but because of controversy surrounding the actress at the time, the studio requested that her costume show less skin. The end result was Travilla's strapless silk creation, worn with matching pink gloves and the eponymous diamonds. Travilla went on to design costumes for eight of the starlet's films, from *The Seven Year Itch* and *How to Marry a Millionaire* to *Bus Stop*.

Travilla
Marilyn Monroe
Diamonds are a girl's Best Friend
Hot Pink

Sabrina
Audrey Hepburn

Sabrina / 1954

Audrey Hepburn

It's no secret that I adore Audrey Hepburn. She has been an enormous source of inspiration for my illustrations over the years. Many of her filmic ensembles became iconic, and this timeless gown is no exception.

The inimitable Hepburn portrayed a chauffer's daughter in Billy Wilder's 1954 film *Sabrina*. Simple and naive Sabrina returns from Paris an enchanting, sophisticated woman and captures the hearts of the wealthy Larrabee brothers. When the two gentlemen, played by Humphrey Bogart and William Holden, see Sabrina upon her return, she is wearing this embroidered bustier ball gown with full skirt. The Larrabee brothers are hooked – and so are we. Edith Head is credited with designing Hepburn's wardrobe and received an Academy Award for Best Costume Design. However, Hubert de Givenchy was rumoured to be responsible for this particular creation, which was chosen personally by Hepburn.

Basic Instinct / 1992

Sharon Stone

Who could forget Sharon Stone's notorious interrogation scene in *Basic Instinct*? When her character, Catherine, is taken for questioning, she makes a quick wardrobe change, but conveniently forgets underwear. Although white usually suggests innocence and purity, those connotations are quickly doused when the heiress provocatively uncrosses her legs.

The minimalist crepe-wool dress, with its polo neck and skin-tight fit, epitomises 1990s chic and was matched with tan heels and Stone's icy-blonde hair. Created by Ellen Mirojnick, the snowy dress is contemporary, timeless and oozes sex appeal, adding to a look that was reminiscent of Alfred Hitchcock's signature femmes fatales. Prior to *Basic Instinct*, Mirojnick designed Gordon Gecko's 'power broker' costumes for 1987's *Wall Street*.

Ellen
Mirojnick
chic
white
dress.
Sharon
Stone
Basic
Instinct

Theoni V. Aldredge
The Great Gatsby
Mia Farrow

The Great Gatsby / 1974

Mia Farrow

One highlight of the 1970s *Great Gatsby* adaptation is Mia Farrow's breathtaking wardrobe. As Daisy Buchanan, the glamorous but self-absorbed socialite, Farrow embraces the jazz age in beaded flapper frocks, fringed accessories, and this silk-chiffon cape and wide-brimmed hat. The gossamer white ensemble beautifully reflects the sunlight, making it perfect for a garden party. The woman behind the look, costume designer Theoni V. Aldredge, had just fifteen days to prepare the film's costumes. While working on *The Great Gatsby*, Aldredge also helped to establish the career of Ralph Lauren, realising his talent and using some of his shirts and suits to dress Robert Redford's Gatsby.

To Catch a Thief / 1955

Grace Kelly

To Catch a Thief must be one of the most stylish movies in the history of Hollywood. Alfred Hitchcock's romance mystery depicts Grace Kelly in ten costumes, each more beautiful than the last. My favourite, however, is this flowing, draped blue gown by Edith Head. The dress, inspired by Dior's 'New Look', features a gathered skirt and variegated chiffon swathes, and was worn with a matching clutch, white open-toe sandals and a floaty blue stole. A bit extravagant? Head designed it that way, befitting Kelly's wealthy, fashionable and vain Frances. At first, Frances acts coldly toward Cary Grant's John – hence the icy blue – but her manner (and her wardrobe) becomes warmer as the two connect. I think I might have watched *To Catch a Thief* a hundred times – still, I never get tired of looking at this dress.

Edith Head
To Catch a Thief
Grace Kelly

Cleopatra
Elizabeth Taylor

Cleopatra / 1963

Elizabeth Taylor

Gazing upon Elizabeth Taylor in Joseph Leo Mankiewicz's 1963 film *Cleopatra*, it's easy to see why she was considered one of the most beautiful women in the world. The epic film saw Taylor don a gilded dress by costume designer Renié Conley, complete with gold headdress, jewellery and 24-carat cape. Designed to look like the wings of a phoenix, the intricate cape was assembled from strips of gold-painted leather and embellished with thousands of beads and sequins. The opulent design won Conley the 1963 Academy Award for Best Costume Design and sold at auction for nearly sixty thousand dollars in 2012.

Arabesque / 1966

Sophia Loren

Gregory Peck and Sophia Loren made for a most glamorous pairing in *Arabesque*. In one scene from the thriller, Loren's character Yasmin lounges in her boudoir wearing this champagne-pink chiffon dress with three-quarter sleeves and tiered ruffles. Designed by Marc Bohan for Christian Dior, the gown appears in the shoe scene, in which the film's villain showers the exotic mistress with beautiful high heels and delivers veiled threats. This wasn't the only memorable fashion moment in the picture. Loren's sumptuous costumes were worth almost fifty thousand dollars and saw *Arabesque* nominated for a BAFTA Award for Best Costume Design. On any other actress this pale-pink gown might have been saccharine, but with Loren's curves it was dangerously seductive.

Christian
Dior
Arabesque
Sophia
Loren

Jacqueline Durran
Anna Karenina
Keira Knightley

Anna Karenina / 2012

Keira Knightley

Keira Knightley donned this lavish jet-black ball gown in *Anna Karenina* for Anna's dance scene with Count Vronsky (Aaron Taylor-Johnson). The actress managed to move effortlessly in the elaborate dress, which had a bustle at the back and layers of draped silk taffeta. The gown comprised sixteen metres of fabric and Knightley had to dance for several days to perfect the scene. Though the film is set in the 1870s, the dress, with its tight bodice and full skirt, was inspired by 1950s haute couture. *Anna Karenina* marked Knightley's third collaboration with costume designer Jacqueline Durran. The duo had previously worked together on *Pride and Prejudice* and *Atonement*, in which Knightley wore another of Durran's lauded creations – the emerald silk evening dress.

Marie Antoinette / 2006

Kirsten Dunst

Working with Kirsten Dunst on a lavish period film shot at the Palace of Versailles sounds like every costume designer's dream, doesn't it? That privilege belonged to Milena Canonero, who designed over sixty candy-coloured frocks for Sofia Coppola's *Marie Antoinette*. One memorable dress is this powder-blue taffeta creation worn with a tricorn – a popular style of hat in the eighteenth century – and a delicate lace and ribbon choker. Canonero's efforts were well rewarded – the veteran costumier won her third Academy Award for Best Costume Design at the Oscars in 2007.

Milena Canonero
Marie Antoinette
Kirsten Dunst

Dina
Bar-El
How to lose
a Guy in 10 days
Canary
Yellow
Kate Hudson

How to Lose a Guy in 10 Days / 2003

Kate Hudson

One vivid scene in the classic romantic comedy *How to Lose a Guy in 10 Days* sees Matthew McConaughey as Ben bombard Andie (Kate Hudson) with a belting rendition of Carly Simon's 'You're So Vain'. Though the confrontation itself is ugly, Andie looks sublime in this canary-yellow silk gown with a revealing neckline and plunging back.

German-born, Beverley Hills–based designer Dina Bar-El dreamt up the stunning floor-length frock, inspired by Andie's 84-carat yellow-diamond pendant. The necklace was reportedly worth over five million dollars – amazingly, it didn't manage to outshine the dress.

Breakfast at Tiffany's / 1961

Audrey Hepburn

You can't stroll past Tiffany's on Fifth Avenue without thinking of the iconic scene in which Audrey Hepburn as Holly Golightly stops on the street to look upon the window display with her coffee and pastry, wearing an utterly sublime LBD. The dress, accessorised with silk gloves, a foot-long cigarette holder and strings of pearls, features a distinctive wing cut at the back and fitted bodice. The dress Hepburn wore in the film was one of several pitched to Paramount. Redesigned by Hollywood costume master Edith Head, the final gown was based on a creation by Hubert de Givenchy. Of all Hepburn's iconic dresses, this one takes the cake. It has resonated with women for over fifty years and will continue to do so for many years to come.

Givenchy
Breakfast at Tiffany's
Audrey Hepburn
Iconic film moment.

Marilyn
Vance
Pretty
Woman
Julia
Roberts

Pretty Woman / 1990

Julia Roberts

Julia Roberts's Vivian makes the transformation from scantily dressed hooker with a heart of gold to elegant society lady in this gorgeously draped, shoulder-baring scarlet dress. Vivian is the centre of attention in the gown as she strolls through the lavish hotel lobby with Richard Gere's Edward. Created by costume designer Marilyn Vance in 1990, the dress might never have made it to screen. The studio originally wanted a black ball gown, but the designer convinced them that a striking red dress was more suited to Vivian's fiery character. The necklace that Roberts wore (presented in that familiar improvised scene in which Edward playfully snaps Vivian's fingers with the lid of the jewellery box) actually did cost $250,000.

Scarface / 1983

Michelle Pfeiffer

Whoever said that crime doesn't pay had obviously never seen Elvira Hancock's wardrobe in *Scarface*. As crime boss Tony Montana's leading lady, Michelle Pfeiffer's Elvira had an endless supply of low-cut gowns bought with her husband's drug money. Think slinky halter dresses and lots of bling, perfect for nights spent chain-smoking and whiling away time at Studio 54. This disco-inspired frock, with its plunging neckline and glitzy sequins, appears in the character's final scene, just before she leaves Tony. Created by costume designer Patricia Norris, the twinkling dress was coupled with Elvira's trademark bob and long, acrylic talons that lived up to her feisty nickname, 'Lady Tiger'. Elvira certainly was a man-eater …

Patricia
Norris
Scarface
Michelle
Pfeiffer

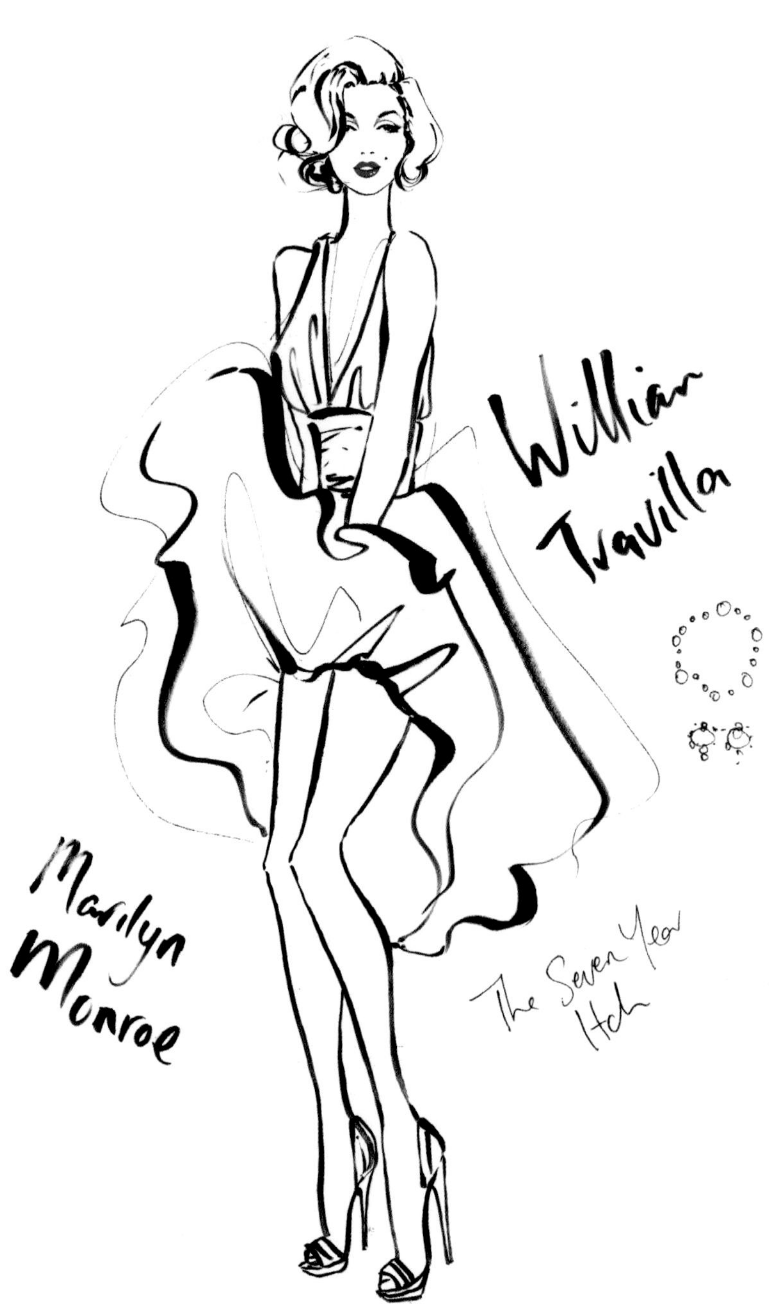
William
Travilla
Marilyn
Monroe
The Seven Year
Itch

The Seven Year Itch / 1955

Marilyn Monroe

Does the dress make the woman or does the woman make the dress? This is surely an example of the latter, although credit where credit is due to costume designer William Travilla, who created the legendary knicker-revealing frock that Marilyn Monroe wore in *The Seven Year Itch*. Who doesn't know that classic image of Monroe standing over the subway grating as her pleated ivory dress billows up around her legs? The halter-style bodice and plunging neckline were very much in vogue during the 1950s and 1960s. Yet Monroe's husband at the time, Joe DiMaggio, is said to have 'hated' the dress – what was he thinking?

Rear Window / 1954

Grace Kelly

In 1954, Alfred Hitchcock recruited Edith Head to design costumes for Grace Kelly, who played a stylish socialite in his film *Rear Window*. Hitchcock's brief to Head was that Kelly 'look like a piece of Dresden china, nearly untouchable'. The outcome was this immortal black and white dress with a fitted bodice, wide neckline and cap sleeves. The layered tulle skirt featured spray bunches embroidered at the waist and was worn with a chiffon wrap, white silk gloves and a pearl necklace and earrings. The V-shaped neckline was kept simple to frame Kelly's face in the famous kissing scene.

It has to be said that this is my favourite film of all time – and my favourite moment is when Grace Kelly enters the room in this dress. I could watch *Rear Window* a thousand times just to see that scene.

Edith Head
Grace Kelly
Rear Window

06 /

Oscar

1955

Grace Kelly

At the 1955 Academy Awards, Grace Kelly received Best Actress for *The Country Girl* and won esteem for her stunning French satin dress, worn with a matching evening coat. Designed by Edith Head, the gown was the most expensive Oscar dress that had ever been made, with the fabric alone costing around four thousand dollars (thirty-five thousand dollars today).

The designer, with whom Kelly had formed a friendship over the years, was known as Hollywood's 'dress doctor'. The actress had worked with Head on *Rear Window* and several other films. 'Some people need sequins – others don't,' Head was quoted as saying at the ceremony, which she attended as Kelly's escort.

Edith Head
1955
Academy Awards
Grace Kelly
Pale Mint

Armani Privé
Silver Sparkling
Anne Hathaway
Fish tail

2009

Anne Hathaway

Armani Privé dressed Anne Hathaway for the 2009 Oscars, where the actress performed a song and dance number with Hugh Jackman to open the show. The *Rachel Getting Married* nominee brought charisma to the red carpet in this strapless gown, hand-picked from Armani's couture collection. The dress featured rays of Swarovski crystals that radiated from the waist and oversized paillettes at the hem. A champagne gown was chosen to match Hathaway's porcelain complexion like a second skin. The colour would prove popular on the night, with other actresses wearing almost identical tones – but no dress stood out like this one.

1999

Gwyneth Paltrow

Gwyneth Paltrow divided fashion watchers with her silk taffeta Ralph Lauren dress at the Academy Awards in 1999. Although some critics were skeptical, the gown is remembered as one of the greatest Oscar dresses of all time. With its demure pink and classic cut, it perfectly embodied Paltrow's gracious persona.

Drawing comparisons to Grace Kelly and inspiring a slew of copycat designs, the influential frock had a full skirt, fitted bodice with spaghetti straps, V-shaped neckline and matching stole. The actress decorated it with $160,000 worth of Harry Winston jewels, gifted to her by her parents. Paltrow was a winner in more ways than one that night, picking up the Best Actress gong for her performance in *Shakespeare in Love.*

Ralph Lauren
Gwyneth Paltrow
Pink Princess Dress

Oscar de La Renta
Amy Adams

2012

Amy Adams

Nominated for an Academy Award for her role in *The Master*, Amy Adams looked to Oscar de la Renta to construct her ball gown. Inspired by an old photograph of a model that she found, Adams pitched the design to de la Renta and collaborated with his team on the garment's every detail. The gown took two weeks to create and the design team were making alterations only hours before Adams walked the red carpet. The flowing result, with its plumage-like chiffon skirt, made Adams every inch the movie star. Looking closely at the skirt's ruffles, one could see tiny 'eyelashes', pulled by hand from each tier.

1998

Sharon Stone

People fussed over Helen Hunt wearing H&M to the 2013 Oscars, but let's go back a few years to 1998. Although rumours circulated about who would dress Sharon Stone for the Oscars, the actress surprised everyone with her cool, casual approach. Mixing high and low fashion, she paired a lilac evening skirt by Vera Wang with a button-down Gap shirt that she nicked from her husband's closet.

The look – refreshing, boyish and distinctively modern – reinvented the white shirt. It wasn't the first time Stone brought her high-meets-low aesthetic to the red carpet. In 1996, she arrived in a Gap turtleneck, which she'd grabbed from her wardrobe in a last-minute dash. Of course, it looked most elegant layered under Valentino and Giorgio Armani.

Gap +
Vera Wang
Sharon
Stone
Gap White
Shirt
with Lilac
Vera Wang
Skirt.

Dior
Beautiful sheer
Sorbet coloured
Gown
Lauren
Hutton
Lilac, pink
mint.

1975

Lauren Hutton

A presenter at the 47th Academy Awards, Lauren Hutton chose this tender creation by Christian Dior. The chiffon dress, featuring Grecian drapery and a pastel ombré spectrum, perfectly complemented her bronze Californian glow. Hutton wore the gown with subtle hair and makeup, a metallic clutch and thin gold belt, which accentuated her waist, in lieu of jewellery. The actress and model had a gorgeous natural look, and like Farrah Fawcett before her, favoured chic simplicity. Lauren Hutton is one of my greatest style inspirations and the best example of 'less is more'.

2005

Hilary Swank

After gaining almost nine kilograms of muscle mass for her role in *Million Dollar Baby*, Hilary Swank showed off her flawless, toned back in this dramatic midnight-blue gown by Guy Laroche. Swank, who collected the Best Actress gong on the night, perfectly balanced the high neckline and long sleeves with the revealing back. Though the design appears simple, the hypnotising dress was created from almost twenty-five metres of silk jersey. The actress, who had planned to wear a Calvin Klein dress, caused some controversy when she changed her mind only weeks before the event. She had seen this Guy Laroche gown on a shopping trip to Paris and just couldn't resist.

Hilary Swank
Guy Laroche
Royal Blue.

Dior
Gisele Bundchen
Strapless Gown

2005

Gisele Bündchen

Trust Gisele Bündchen to steal the spotlight from *The Aviator* star and Best Actor nominee Leonardo DiCaprio at the Oscars in 2005. Accompanying her beau, the Victoria's Secret supermodel wore a voluminous white dress with sequined embroidery by John Galliano for Christian Dior, launching a trend toward fuller silhouettes that lasted for seasons. Bündchen looked every bit the goddess in the empire-waisted Grecian number, proving that a skin-tight fit is not always best. The model, who would look great in a brown paper bag, revitalised the red carpet that year with her fresh take on the classic cut.

2001

Renée Zellweger

Renée Zellweger wore a relatively unknown designer to the 2001 Academy Awards. This canary-yellow Jean Dessès gown, which Zellweger found in a vintage boutique, was flattering and chic and distinguished the emerging actress for her sense of style. Jean Dessès was a mid-century designer known for dressing royals and celebrities and for mentoring Valentino. When Zellweger discovered the dress at Beverly Hills vintage store Lily et Cie, it was nearly fifty years old. And yet the gown hadn't aged a day. The design was timeless and the star was jubilant about her choice: 'It's old and it fit and I love it,' she said.

Canary yellow
No 5
Renée Zellweger
Vintage Jean Dessès

Cate Blanchett
Givenchy by Riccardo Tisci

2011

Cate Blanchett

Never one to shy away from a red-carpet gamble, Cate Blanchett looked phenomenal at the 2011 Academy Awards in this lilac and yellow Riccardo Tisci for Givenchy gown. The exceptional garment was constructed from two components – a pleated halter dress and an embellished breast piece with geometric shoulders, which was made of elastic and could be separated from the dress. The gown was part of Givenchy's 2011 couture collection, which was inspired by the unlikely combination of Japanese robot toys and Butoh, a style of contemporary dance. Blanchett wears couture with total éclat, making her a muse for designer Riccardo Tisci: 'People like Cate are the reason I do what I do.'

1988

Cher

As well as for singing and acting her way to the top, Cher will always be remembered for her show-stopping fashion choices. And none of them were bolder than this sheer black dress by American designer Bob Mackie, which Cher wore when she defeated Meryl Streep to win the Best Actress Oscar for *Moonstruck*. Beating Meryl is a feat in itself! And what better way to show off her taut stomach and legs than this body-baring creation, featuring thin straps and a lacy décolleté?

Cher and Mackie worked together over four decades, tallying up several notable fashion moments between them. Cher was honoured in 1992 by Madame Tussauds as one of the five most beautiful women in history. Her wax figure wears a replica of this fabulous Bob Mackie creation. You know that you've made it when they erect you in wax!

Bob Mackie
Cher
Daring black beaded creation

Vera Wang
Keira Knightley
Oscar dress
Dark plum.
One shoulder
gown.

2006

Keira Knightley

Keira Knightley embraced old-school Hollywood glamour at the 78th Academy Awards, where she was nominated for Best Actress for her role in *Pride and Prejudice*. The Brit, who wanted something dramatic and sexy, selected the silk-taffeta fishtail gown by Vera Wang and paired it with a multicoloured necklace by Bulgari. Knightley, though poised, still managed to look young and fresh. Critics cited the burgundy frock as one of the best Oscar dresses of all time and a Debenhams poll voted it the sixth greatest red-carpet gown in history. After the ceremony, Knightley donated the dress to Oxfam International. At auction, it raised almost eight thousand dollars, which went toward alleviating the food crisis in East Africa. A beautiful ending to a beautiful dress.

2001

Julia Roberts

Although couture, the black and white gown that Julia Roberts wore when she collected her Best Actress Oscar for *Erin Brockovich* was not custom made. The Valentino creation was actually part of a 1992 collection and was pulled from the archives for Roberts. Widely praised by fashion critics, the slinky black dress with white piping was intended to evoke classic Hollywood, inspired by luminaries such as Elizabeth Taylor and Jackie Kennedy. When Roberts spotted the frock, which was returned to Valentino's archives, she reportedly said, 'I just thought it was a pretty dress.' Valentino Garavani has cited the moment Roberts won Best Actress as the high point of his fifty-year career.

Julia Roberts
Valentino
Dramatic Black with Signature white Stripe.

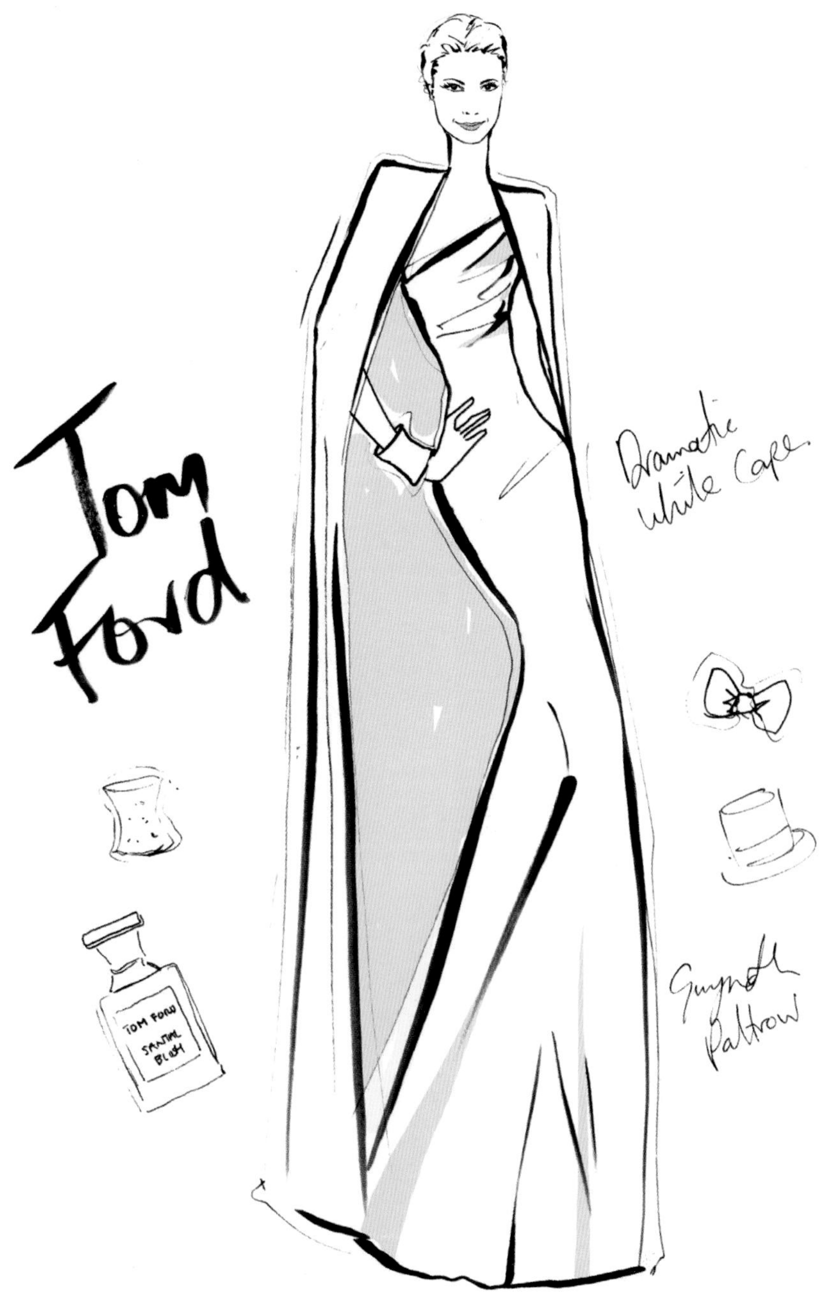
Tom Ford
Dramatic white cape.
Gwyneth Paltrow
TOM FORD SANTAL BLUSH

2012

Gwyneth Paltrow

At the 2012 Academy Awards, Gwyneth Paltrow wowed in this floor-length cape by Tom Ford. The ivory ensemble was part of the designer's secretive Fall collection, which was not even shown at London Fashion Week – Paltrow's appearance at the Oscars was the public's first glimpse of it. The arresting gown had an asymmetrical neckline and Paltrow complemented it with an Anna Hu diamond cuff and ring, Jimmy Choo shoes and a sleek ponytail. The cape has since caught on – *12 Years a Slave* actress Lupita Nyong'o wore a similar dress in red to the 2014 Golden Globes. Could the tasteful cape guarantee your spot on the best-dressed list? Without question.

2007

Nicole Kidman

At the 2007 Academy Awards, Nicole Kidman took a chance with this stunning vermillion gown by Nicolas Ghesquière for Balenciaga. A longtime fan of the designer, Kidman had worn Balenciaga for her wedding to Keith Urban the previous year. Critics raved over Kidman's halter dress, which featured a plush bow at the nape that draped elegantly down into a train. It's a daring move to wear red on the red carpet, and only a special design will remain distinctive. Miraculously, this striking dress not only stood out, it was the clear favourite in a sea of predictable awards-season frocks.

Balenciaga
Nicole Kidman

Edith Head
Audrey Hepburn

1954

Audrey Hepburn

Audrey Hepburn and Hubert de Givenchy were a match made in sartorial heaven. The doyenne of the screen and the French designer, who were close in age, empathised with one another and shared an intimate relationship that lasted into old age. Hepburn called Givenchy her best friend and Givenchy referred to her as a sister. The couturier intuitively understood the star's petite frame and designed sophisticated and simple dresses that enhanced her tiny waist and swan-like neck. This ivory lace dress, which Hepburn wore to accept her Best Actress Oscar for *Roman Holiday*, was the first Givenchy design that she wore in public. The belted gown was reportedly adapted from an Edith Head creation that the actress sported in the final scene of the film. Hepburn later referred to it as her 'lucky' dress and *Time* magazine named it the Best Oscar Dress of All Time.

Acknowledgements

To Paul McNally for creating another dream book with me and giving me the freedom to illustrate on a topic that I was so passionate about.

To Meelee Soorkia for being a wonderful editor and making the whole process so much fun. I feel like we've created the perfect couture wardrobe together! (You can keep the meat dress.)

To Martina Granolic for being my 'Fashion Yoda' and meticulously going through many hundreds of dresses to hone the perfect final list with me.

To Jo Barry for your incredible research into every single dress in this book. I have no doubt that if you ever decide to change careers, you would make an incredible private eye.

To Justine Clay for encouraging and supporting my work from the early days. Any wonderful projects that have come my way are because of you.

To Candace Bushnell for not only giving me my first big break, but also your ongoing advice and friendship, which has given me more confidence in my work than you will ever know.

And finally, to my family. To my little boy Will for sitting on my wardrobe floor playing with his Hot Wheels cars while I get dressed – when I look at you I know what really matters in life. To my daughter Gwyn for her sage fashion advice: 'Only wear jumpsuits if people can really tell that they're not pyjamas.' And to my husband Craig for being my partner in crime and building me the ultimate wardrobe. Now we just need to fill it with every dress in this book!

About the author

Megan Hess was destined to draw. Her initial career as a graphic designer led to her employment as an art director at some of the world's leading design agencies. In 2008, Megan illustrated Candace Bushnell's *New York Times* bestseller *Sex and the City*. She has since illustrated portraits for *Vanity Fair* and *Time* magazines, created iconic works of art for Cartier of Paris, and decorated the windows of Bergdorf Goodman in New York.

Megan also channels this signature style into her bespoke range of silk scarves and limited-edition prints, which are sold around the globe. Her illustrious clients include Chanel, Dior, Tiffany & Co., Yves Saint Laurent, *Vogue*, *Harper's Bazaar*, Cartier, Ladurée and the Ritz Hotel in Paris.

When she's not working in her studio, Megan is usually hiding in a coffee shop, secretly sketching those around her and looking for that perfectly dressed person – perhaps, in the perfect dress.

Visit Megan at meganhess.com

Published in 2014 by Hardie Grant Books

Hardie Grant Books (Australia)
Ground Floor, Building 1
658 Church Street
Richmond, Victoria 3121
www.hardiegrant.com.au

Hardie Grant Books (UK)
Dudley House, North Suite
34–35 Southampton Street
London WC2E 7HF
www.hardiegrant.co.uk

A Cataloguing-in-Publication entry is available from the catalogue of the National Library of Australia at www.nla.gov.au

The Dress: 100 Iconic Moments in Fashion
ISBN: 978 1 74270 823 2

Publishing Director: Paul McNally
Project Editor: Meelee Soorkia
Editor: Milly Main
Researcher: Jo Barry
Design Manager: Mark Campbell
Concept Designer: Murray Batten
Typesetter: Megan Ellis
Production Manager: Todd Rechner

Colour reproduction by Splitting Image Colour Studio

Printed in China by 1010 Printing International Limited

Draped in Sheer Silk
Tailored to perfection